DANCE

BALLROOM DANCING

by Joan Freese

Consultant:
Dance Fever Studio
Needham, Massachusetts

Capstone press

Mankato, Minnesota

Snap Books are published by Capstone Press,
151 Good Counsel Drive, P.O. Box 669, Mankato, Minnesota 56002.
www.capstonepress.com

Library of Congress Cataloging-in-Publication Data

Freese, Joan.
    Ballroom dancing / Joan Freese.
    p. cm.—(Snap books. Dance)
    Summary: "Describes ballroom dancing, including history, training,
moves, and competition"—Provided by publisher.
    Includes bibliographical references and index.
    ISBN-13: 978-1-4296-0123-8 (hardcover)
    ISBN-10: 1-4296-0123-X (hardcover)
    1. Ballroom dancing—Juvenile literature. I. Title. II. Series.
GV1751.F75 2008
793.3'3—dc22   2006102784

Editor: Becky Viaene

Designer: Veronica Bianchini

Photo Researcher: Laura Manthe

Photo Credits:

Associated Press/Wong Maye-E, 12–13; Associated Press/WWD, 14 (top); Capstone Press/Karon Dubke, front cover, back
cover, 7, 8 (shoes), 9, 11, 14 (bottom), 19, 20–21, 27, 29; Corbis/Reuters/Luis Enrique Ascui, 25 (dancers); Courtesy of
author Joan Freese, 32; iStockphoto/Cloudytronics, 5 (top); iStockphoto/Kenneth C. Zirkel, 2–3; Picture This Vancouver
Canada/Andrew Leung, 22–23, 31; Shutterstock/Filipchuk Oleg Vladimirovich, 15 (right); Shutterstock/Gina Goforth,
8 (dancers); Shutterstock/Jaimie Duplass, 5 (couple with hat); Shutterstock/Jian Bin Ping, 17; Shutterstock/Vallentin
Vassileff, 6 (dancers), 15 (left), 18 (dancers), 22 (dancers), 26 (dancers)

Acknowledgements:
**Joan Freese would like to thank the ballroom instructors who helped with this book, especially Raisa
Bernsten and Nathan Daniels of Magic Ballroom in St. Louis Park, Minnesota, and Frances Emberley at
Cinema Ballroom in Saint Paul, Minnesota.** Capstone Press thanks the Arthur Murray Dance Center in Saint
Paul, Minnesota, for their assistance with this book.

Table of Contents

Chapter 1

The Beauty of Ballroom 4

Chapter 2

Beginning Ballroom 6

Chapter 3

Starting with Standard 10

Chapter 4

Loving Latin Dances 16

Chapter 5

Taking the Next Step 24

Glossary 30

Fast Facts 30

Read More 31

Internet Sites 31

About the Author 32

Index 32

Chapter One

THE BEAUTY OF BALLROOM

You hear the beautiful music. You see flashes of color as dancers whisk by in elegant costumes. You feel the rhythm and want to join in the fun.

Yet ballroom dancing offers more than just smooth moves and amazing costumes. It builds confidence and teamwork skills. Ballroom dancing also offers exercise while improving your balance, flexibility, and coordination.

From weddings to competitions, ballroom dancing is something that people of all ages can enjoy. So why wait? Start taking lessons so you can move across the ballroom dance floor with style and grace.

Chapter Two

BEGINNING BALLROOM

Before you can become great at any type of dance, you need to understand the dance.

You can learn about ballroom dancing by watching movies like *Mad Hot Ballroom* or instructional videos. But doing is better than watching. So the best way to learn ballroom dancing is to take a class.

You might be surprised to discover that in your beginning ballroom class, you may not even dance with a partner. No worries! There's plenty to learn about each dance before you put the moves together as a couple.

Pretty for Practice

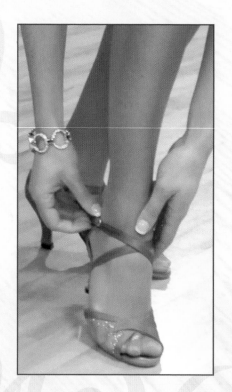

Clothes for ballroom dance class should be comfortable. You'll likely be dancing up a sweat, so short-sleeve shirts are your best bet. Clothes should fit close to your body so the instructor can tell if you're doing the positions correctly. But everyday jeans are too tight to let you move freely. Many people dress up for class by wearing dress pants or long flowing skirts.

The most important part of your outfit is shoes. Leave your sneakers at home. Women wear dance shoes with straps and short heels. Men wear black lightweight leather shoes with short heels. Smooth-soled dance shoes help pairs glide across a dance floor.

Stretching

So you made it to class. Now what? Start by stretching to prevent injuries.
Try simple stretches, such as neck rolls, arm circles, ankle circles, and toe touches.
Take your time, remembering to warm up every part of your body.

Starting With Standard

You'll quickly find that each type of ballroom dance is unique.

Ballroom dancing is split into International and American. International is faster and more competitive and is the focus of this book.

Your first ballroom dance classes will probably focus on standard style.

Standard dances include the waltz, Viennese waltz, fox trot, quickstep, and tango. These dances first became popular in Austria, the United States, England, and Argentina. Standard dances are called progressive because couples move counterclockwise around the floor.

Positions Please

The most common position in standard ballroom dancing is the closed position. Partners stand facing each other, with the woman slightly to the right of the man. The man's right hand is on the woman's back, between her waist and shoulder blades. The woman's left hand rests on the man's right shoulder. The man bends his left arm at the elbow. The woman places her right hand between his thumb and index finger.

Waltz

Grab your gown and get ready to waltz. First danced in Austria, the waltz is a widely popular dance. Knowing how to dance the waltz will make other dances easier to learn. The first step of this elegant dance is the strongest. Think: **1**, 2, 3, **1**, 2, 3. The dancer's first step is done on a flat foot. The next two steps are done quickly on the balls of the feet. The first step also includes a slight turn. The combination of turns and the rise and fall motion gives the waltz a graceful look.

Viennese Waltz

Ready to speed things up? Try the waltz again, but this time do it twice as fast and with plenty of turns. This whirling dance is called the Viennese waltz. This waltz is the fastest and oldest of all competitive ballroom dances. It became popular in Vienna, Austria, in the mid-1700s. You could say it's the grandparent of all ballroom dances!

Letting Him Lead

Be a polite partner. Women, resist the urge to lead—even if you do know the dance better than your partner. Being the lead isn't an easy job. Men lead by deciding what move to do next and letting their partners know without talking. Plus it's also the man's responsibility to watch the traffic flow on the dance floor so couples don't collide.

Fox Trot

In 1914, audiences in the United States watched actor Harry Fox's smooth dancing style. His dance quickly caught on and was soon called the fox trot. By the 1930s, famous dancers like Fred Astaire and Ginger Rogers were dancing the fox trot too. When dancers fox trot, they slide smoothly across the floor in a slow-slow-quick-quick rhythm.

Quickstep

Faster! Faster! In the 1920s, bands were playing fox trot music too fast to dance to. In England, a fast fox trot and a dance called the Charleston were combined to create the quickstep. The quickstep keeps dancers on their toes with quick steps, hops, and even short runs. Its energy makes the dance fun to watch.

Tango

The tango is a romantic dance that's often called "the dance of love." This dramatic tango became popular in Buenos Aires, Argentina, in the late 1800s. For this dance, partners stand very close in closed position. The basic tango combines the five steps of slow-slow-quick-quick-slow.

Chapter Four

Loving Latin Dances

After learning some standard dances, you may want to start spicing up the ballroom with Latin dances.

The samba, paso doble, rumba, cha-cha, and jive will soon have you moving your feet and your hips. These flashy, dramatic dances first became popular in Brazil, Spain, Cuba, and the United States.

Latin dances are different from standard dances in several ways. For Latin dances, couples are not always in the closed position. Most Latin dances are done in place, instead of moving counterclockwise around the floor. Also, dancers often dress in flashier costumes for Latin dances.

Samba

Colorfully dressed people celebrate at the annual Carnival in Brazil by dancing the samba in the streets. This exciting dance became popular in Rio de Janeiro, Brazil, in the late 1800s. The lively moves of the samba soon spread to other countries. The steps of the samba are quick, with obvious hip movements. These movements come from bending and straightening the knees. The basic samba steps have a small bounce and can be danced forward-back or side-to-side.

Paso Doble

The paso doble is meant to look like a bullfight. This dance began in Spain and was quickly spreading to other countries by the 1920s. During this dramatic dance, the man uses sharp marching moves to imitate the bullfighter. The woman uses light and flowing moves to represent the red cape.

Rumba

The rumba is a flirty dance that may look like a game of cat and mouse. The woman gets close to the man and then moves quickly away.

Workers in the farm fields of Cuba created this exciting dance, which came to the United States in the late 1920s. The rumba combines slow, smooth moves with a rolling of the hips.

Don't Say Cheese

During most ballroom dances you want to smile and look happy, but not for the rumba. The rumba has a more serious feel, so save the smile for another dance.

Cha-Cha

Here is another flirty, fun dance that became popular in Cuba. In the 1950s, couples were making moves similar to the mambo, but quicker. The lively dance called the cha-cha-cha was the new craze. Dancers couldn't wait to get on the floor and try the dance's slow, slow, quick, quick, quick pattern of moves. The dance's name was later shortened to the cha-cha, but the moves, including small steps and quick turns, stayed the same.

Jive

Get ready for some serious fun because it's time to jive. This fast dance became popular in the United States in the 1930s. American soldiers brought the dance to Europe during World War II (1939–1945). The jive is a combination of dances. Lifts, jumps, and acrobatics are all part of the jive.

TAKING THE NEXT STEP

After lots of practicing, you may want to dance for more than just fun.

Ballroom dance competitions are held each year across the United States and worldwide. Competitions, often called DanceSport, follow the rules of the International DanceSport Federation (IDSF) and the World Dance Council (WDC).

At competitions, couples gather to compete against other pairs. Dancers are divided by age into groups of pre-teen (9–11), junior (12–15), youth (16–18), and adult (19+, 35+, and 50+). Dancers compete in standard or Latin and must be prepared to dance any of the dances in their category.

An Elegant Outfit

If you enter ballroom dance competitions, you'll need to pay more attention to what you wear. That's because most ballroom competitions have strict dress codes.

For females, the dress code differs depending on competitors' ages. Girls younger than 16 must wear simple dresses with no sequins, feathers, or fringes. They wear very little makeup. Women who are older than 16 wear bright makeup and decorated costumes. Despite the costume differences, both women and girls should put their hair back in a bun.

For boys and men the dress code is the same. Dark dress pants, plain white dress shirts, ties, and dance shoes make the outfit complete. To look even sharper, some men wear tuxedos and bow ties. On competition day, each man is given a number to pin on the back of his shirt. This number is used by the judges.

27

Competition Judging

Ballroom dance competitions are your chance to show how well you can do the moves. You and your partner will begin by competing each dance against about 12 other couples. You'll only have about two minutes to wow the judges. After each dance, three to five judges narrow it down to six couples.

Judging is based on many things, including posture, timing, appearance, difficulty of moves, and enthusiasm.

Throughout the competition, you'll probably perform four different types of dances. The top three overall winning couples are awarded a cash prize or a trophy.

Whether you compete or not, the most important part of ballroom dancing is having fun. From the waltz to the cha-cha, ballroom dancing is a skill that you can use for years to come.

Competition Tips

*Some extra things to bring on competition day include safety pins, hairspray, and a towel. Use the towel to wipe sweat from your forehead. And if the strap on your dress breaks, safety pins might save the day.

*Be ready and waiting at least 30 minutes before you need to compete.

*If you make a mistake, keep smiling and moving, and don't blame your partner!

Glossary

closed position (KLOHZD puh-ZISH-uhn)—a dance position in which dancers face and hold each other

coordination (koh-or-duh-NAY-shuhn)—good control over the movement of arms and legs

posture (POSS-chur)—the position of your body

progressive (pruh-GRESS-iv)—moving forward or happening steadily; standard style ballroom dances are progressive.

rhythm (RITH-um)—a regular beat in music or dance

timing (TIM-ing)—the ability to choose the right moment to do something; couples are judged on their timing with the music and each other.

Fast Facts

Around the 1930s, Fred Astaire and Ginger Rogers showed their incredible ballroom dancing talent in ten Hollywood musicals. Astaire even co-founded a chain of ballroom dance studios that still exist today.

Each year, almost 50,000 couples from 75 countries perform in ballroom dancing competitions.

National Ballroom Dance Week is celebrated each year in the United States September 14–19.

One of the largest ballroom dance competitions in the world is called the Ohio Star Ball. It is held each year in Columbus, Ohio, and is only for the best dancers.

Read More

Bottomer, Paul. *Ballroom Dancing: Step-by-Step.* London: Southwater, 2007.

Gillis, Jennifer Blizin. *Ballroom Dancing for Fun!* Minneapolis: Compass Point Books, 2008.

Zimmerer, Eric. *Shall We Dance: A Beginner's Guide to Ballroom Dancing.* Sunnyvale, Calif.: Ace of Hearts, 2003.

Internet Sites

FactHound offers a safe, fun way to find Internet sites related to this book. All of the sites on FactHound have been researched by our staff.

Here's how:

1. Visit *www.facthound.com*

2. Choose your grade level.

3. Type in this book ID **142960123X** for age-appropriate sites. You may also browse subjects by clicking on letters, or by clicking on pictures and words.

4. Click on the **Fetch It** button.

Facthound will fetch the best sites for you!

About the Author

Joan Freese's first job out of college was in the press office of American Ballet Theatre in New York City. Next she worked as a copy editor for *Dance Ink* and as associate editor of *The Poor Dancer's Almanac*, published by Duke University Press. Her articles on dance have appeared in *Dance Magazine*, *The Village Voice*, and the *Star Tribune*. She has also written extensively for kids on a variety of topics. Joan dedicates this book to her son August.

INDEX

classes, 6, 8, 10
clothes,
    for competitions,
        4, 16, 26
    for practice, 8
competitions, 24, 26,
    28, 29

International
    DanceSport
        Federation, 24

judging, 26, 28

Latin style, 16–22, 24
    cha-cha, 16, 21,
        28
    jive, 16, 22
    paso doble, 16, 19
    rumba, 16, 20
    samba, 16, 18

standard style, 10–15,
    24
    fox trot, 10, 14
    quickstep, 10, 14
    tango, 10, 15
    Viennese waltz,
        10, 13
    waltz, 10, 12, 13,
        28

World Dance
    Council, 24

WATCHUNG LIBRARY
12 STIRLING ROAD
WATCHUNG, NJ 07069